# Santa's Wish

*How a little girl's thoughtfulness gives Santa hope that his secret wish will soon come true.*

By:
## "K" Stone

"K" Stone

Illustrated By:
## Mary Lee Dunn

Send Santa a thank-you
Pictures or words will
do! ♡, +
CB

Halo ●●●●
Publishing International

ISBN 13: 978-1-61244-468-0
Library of Congress Control Number: 2016913868

Printed in the United States of America

Halo ● ● ●
Publishing International
www.halopublishing.com

Published by Halo Publishing International
1100 NW Loop 410
Suite 700 - 176
San Antonio, Texas 78213
Toll Free 1-877-705-9647
www.halopublishing.com
www.holapublishing.com
e-mail: contact@halopublishing.com

# Santa's Secret Wish

### Story by "K" Stone

### With illustrations by Mary Lee Dunn

# DEDICATION

## FOR

## ALL WHO HAVE GRATEFUL HEARTS

# ACKNOWLEDGEMENTS

**Manon Romash** — a friend and former student who assisted with her expert computer skills

**Ginny Matish** — a friend whose support and suggestions were invaluable in creating this book

**Debbie Baxter** — a friend, fellow writer, and former English teacher who edited my story

SANTA CLAUS

JING-A-LING-A-LING!!! Bells rang out the five minute warning for Santa's sleigh to lift off on Christmas Eve. Santa was busy writing Charlotte's letter to be placed in her stocking that very night. He knew that she was a great swimmer, but he only had enough time to praise her good manners and her helpful ways. Santa quickly sealed the letter and put it in his bulging mail bag. Santa had begun writing letters to really good children many years ago, and he'd always hoped to receive lots of mail **after** Christmas.

Quickly, he jumped on the jam-packed sleigh, clicked the reins, and rose into the starry sky. When his long night of landing on roof tops, squeezing down chimneys, stuffing stockings, and eating tasty treats came to an end, he returned to the North Pole for a well-deserved rest.

Winter vacation had always been a happy, relaxing time for Santa, but not this year. He was so-o-o sad! Nothing could turn over his tickle box! No "HO, HO, HO's" left his lips. Just like every other January, Mrs. Claus cooked his favorite foods, and Jack Frost had dressed the North Pole in a bright white coat of beautiful snow. But Santa was still not happy. Neither the elves nor Mrs. Claus could figure out why he was down in the dumps. They were really worried about poor, sad Santa.

Every day Santa moped around the house. After lunch, he trudged to his mail box hoping to find some letters. As he walked, he wondered out loud, "Did Michael like the soccer ball I substituted for the baseball, and was Violet feeling safer at bedtime with the surprise rainbow light I left her?" Santa eased open the mail box. EMPTY AGAIN!

Santa walked back home as Mrs. Claus watched through the window. She didn't see the frozen tear trails on Santa's chubby cheeks until he sat in his comfy chair.

Soon, Santa's most loyal elf CB dropped by for a visit. He too, had watched Santa "be blue" for days. He asked Santa, "Why are you so sad? I've never seen you like this before."

Santa spoke slowly, "I have a secret wish! I want to get a stack of letters *after* Christmas that's as high as the pile I get *before* Christmas. When I started leaving letters in children's stockings, I thought for sure I'd get some mail after Christmas, but I've never received any letters."

CB asked, "So you want to know if you are doing a good job making children happy, right?"

"Right, and I want to get to know the children better," said Santa.

CB waved a quick good-bye. He knew a special little girl who could put a smile back on Santa's face. CB had been Charlotte and her sister's elf for years. He recalled how much Charlotte loved to make cards. He took off at once to find her!

When CB found Charlotte, she was in the upstairs playroom at her grandmother KK's house. She had finished making thank you cards for Trey, Chris, Barbara, Kirk, and Ninnie. She was also making Santa a card. CB knew it would not be many days before Santa would find a letter. He headed home amazed by Charlotte's thoughtfulness.

After finishing her card, Charlotte took it downstairs to show KK who was busy in the kitchen. "KK, can we mail this letter when you take me home?" asked Charlotte.

"Let's address it first," KK said.

Charlotte was proud of her card, and she asked KK if she thought Santa would like it. KK replied, "It is so sparkly; I know he will!"

Back at the North Pole, Santa continued to check his mail box daily. Still no mail came! One really windy, cold day, Santa did not want to go. Mrs. Claus said, "A walk in the fresh air will do you good." Santa knew she was right, so he went. The mailbox was frozen closed. Santa strained to open its door. When he looked inside, he saw a letter. He grabbed the envelope in his freezing fingers and danced a jig all the way up the lane. When back inside, Santa eagerly read Charlotte's letter. Her words warmed his heart. Santa was so proud of his thank you note. He kept it in his pocket so he could read it again and again.

Santa wanted to do something really special for Charlotte because she had given him back his joy. He sent for CB and said, "Please deliver this invitation to Charlotte." CB went straight to Charlotte's bedroom that night and slipped the invitation under her pillow.

The next morning when she found it, she ran into her parents' room begging, "Can I go, please, please?"

Barely awake, Daddy said, "Settle down now and tell us **where** and **when** you want to go."

Charlotte was jumping around joyfully as she answered, "To New York, to ride on Santa's float in Macy's Thanksgiving Day Parade! Oh, *please, please, please,* may I go?" Charlotte could see confusion on her parents' faces, so she handed them Santa's invitation.

Charlotte's parents were surprised and so excited for their daughter. They reassured her by saying, "We will contact Macy's Thanksgiving Day Parade officials and make all the arrangements."

The many months crawled by. Thanksgiving Day finally arrived. The Stone family took an early flight to New York. The parade officials met them at the airport and took them to the float. When Charlotte stepped out of the limo, she felt like a celebrity. She was a bit nervous, but when she heard Santa's voice the fun began. As Santa leaned over to shake Charlotte's hand, she gave him a kiss on the cheek. "Next to my daddy, you are my favorite man!" she exclaimed.

"I really appreciated your thank you letter after Christmas," Santa said smiling. "I hope I get lots more so my secret wish will come true."

Surprised, Charlotte asked, "What is your secret wish, Santa?"

"To get a stack of mail from children **after** Christmas that is as tall as the stack I get **before** Christmas," Santa answered. "After Christmas, I would have time to enjoy the letters, and I could find out if I made children happy. After all, bringing joy to every girl and boy is my job!"

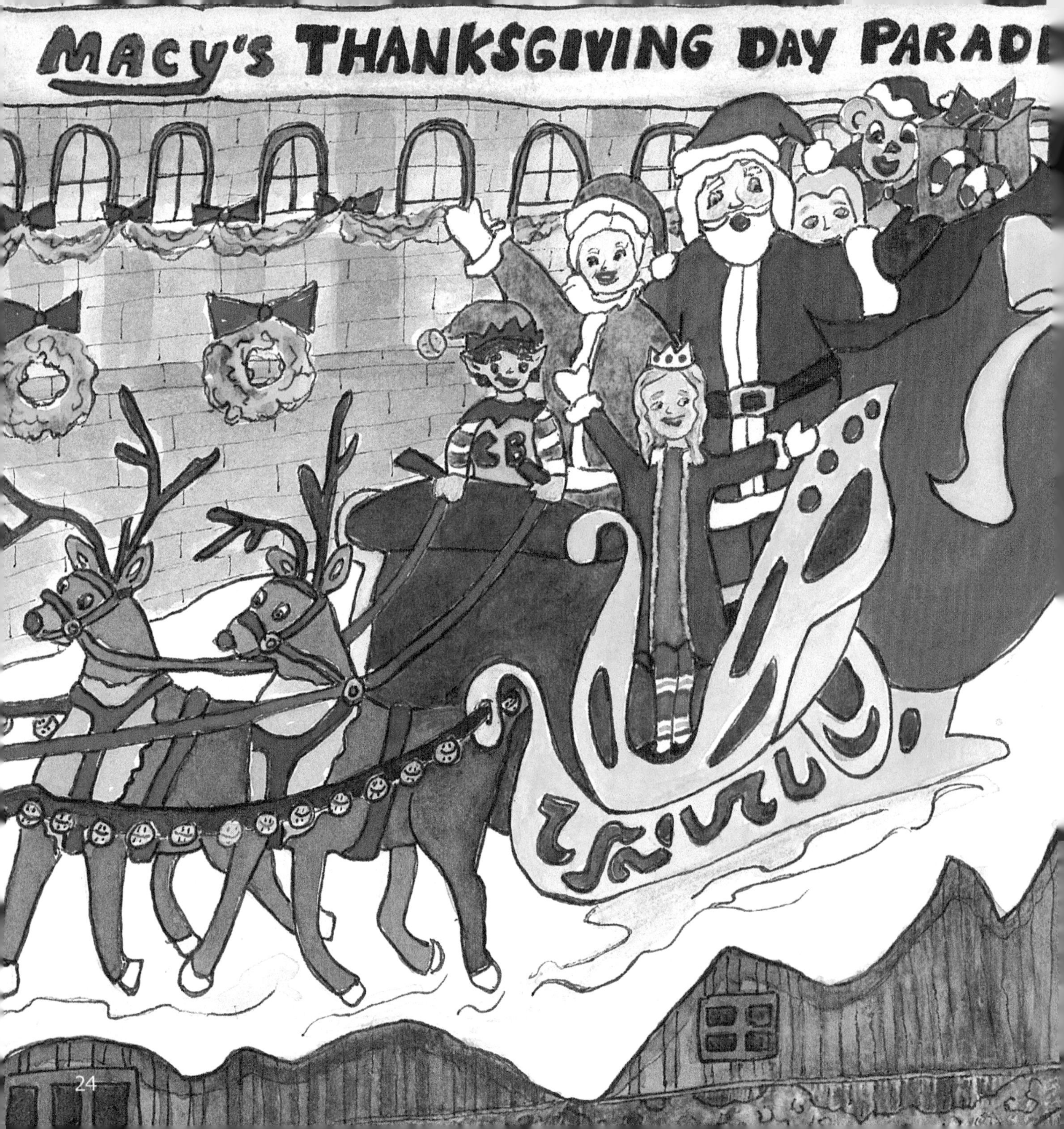
MACY'S THANKSGIVING DAY PARADE
CB

Later, Charlotte climbed onto Santa's float for the parade to begin. The sky was filled with huge, colorful balloons, as beautiful floats moved slowly down Sixth Avenue. Santa's float was always last, and every year it got the most applause from the crowds. Charlotte loved waving to the people cheering for Santa. She smiled so much her jaws hurt! It was the happiest day of her life. When the parade ended, Santa rushed to the North Pole to prepare for Christmas Eve deliveries.

When Charlotte got off the float, a newspaper reporter was anxious to talk to her. The reporter's first question was, "Did one of your parents suggest that you write a thank you note to Santa, or did you come up with the idea on your own?"

Charlotte answered, "When I started my thank you notes, the idea just popped into my mind. Santa does give me the most gifts! Also, the letters he leaves in my stocking make me want to do good things."

"Well, Charlotte, you may not know it," the reporter said, "but **YOU** gave Santa the best gift of all, that wonderful feeling of being **appreciated**. Now, he knows for certain that he is doing a great job!"

If you would like to help make Santa's secret wish come true, use this stationery to write a letter to him.

Dear Santa,

CPSIA information can be obtained
at www.ICGtesting.com
Printed in the USA
BVOW07s2315140916
462172BV00008B/17/P